RAPHAEL

A Biography by
ELIZABETH RIPLEY

PURPLE HOUSE PRESS
Kentucky

Art History Biographies from
Elizabeth Ripley

**BOTTICELLI
GOYA
LEONARDO DA VINCI
MICHELANGELO
REMBRANDT
RUBENS
TITIAN
VINCENT VAN GOGH
WINSLOW HOMER**

JUSTICE, c. 1509
Vatican, Rome

Title page: **SAINT GEORGE AND THE DRAGON**, c. 1503-1505, Louvre, Paris
Painting titles are taken from the museums where they reside and may differ from the 1961 edition

Published by Purple House Press, PO Box 787, Cynthiana, Kentucky 41031
Classic Living Books for Kids and Young Adults, purplehousepress.com

Written in 1961 by Elizabeth Ripley
Text is unabridged, with corrections for historical accuracy.
Revised edition copyright © 2022 by Purple House Press
All rights reserved   ISBN 9781948959957

Illustrations

1 Saint George and the Dragon
2 Justice
5 The Knight's Dream
7 Drawing for Coronation of Saint Nicholas of Tolentino
9 The Crucifixion
11 Marriage of the Virgin
13 Self-Portrait
15 Madonna of the Grand Duke
17 Entombment Drawing
19 Entombment
21 Saint George
23 Madonna of the Meadow
25 Agnolo Doni
25 Maddalena Doni
27 Drawings for Madonna of the Goldfinch
29 Madonna of the Goldfinch
31 La Belle Jardinière
33 Sketches for Disputa
35 Dispute of the Holy Sacrament (Disputa)
37 School of Athens
39 Poetry
41 Parnassus
43 The Mass at Bolsena
45 Heliodorus Chased from the Temple
47 Meeting of Saint Leo and Attila
49 Deliverance of Saint Peter
51 Madonna of the Chair
53 Galatea
55 Fire in Borgo
57 Miraculous Draught of Fishes
59 Baldassare Castiglione
61 Sistine Madonna
63 Leo X with Cardinals Medici and Rossi
65 Heads and Hands of Apostles
67 Transfiguration

RAPHAEL SANTI held his father's hand as they climbed the narrow street leading from their house to the Duke of Urbino's castle. He could see the pointed caps of the castle's towers soaring into the blue sky. In a few days Duke Guidobaldo was to be married, Giovanni Santi told his son. He was on his way to discuss the pageant which the duke had asked him to design.

Father and son paused at the top of the hill to look out on overlapping mountains stretching to the sea. Then they walked through a gateway into the courtyard of the most beautiful palace in Italy. Giovanni led his son through rooms bright with gayly colored tapestries and paintings, until they came to the library where the duke sat reading. Guidobaldo rose to greet his court painter. He rested his hand on Raphael's curly head. This child was well named for the angel Raphael, he thought.

Raphael loved to visit the duke's castle. Sometimes Guidobaldo let him look at illustrated books, or he sat by his father while he painted a portrait of some lord or lady. He watched how Giovanni held his brush and how he mixed two colors together to make a third. Soon Raphael learned to paint little pictures of his own. Giovanni showed them to the duke, who was impressed by the child's talent.

When Raphael was eleven years old his father caught a fever. A few days later he died. The duke and duchess, saddened by the loss of their favorite court painter, were eager to help Giovanni's son to become an artist. Since his mother had died when he was eight years old they talked to the boy's uncle about his nephew's education, and one day in 1494 Raphael entered the workshop of Timoteo Viti. He learned quickly.

Years later the duchess was charmed by his peaceful little pictures painted in clear fresh colors. There was one of winged Saint Michael spearing the dragon, another of three dancing nymphs, and a third of an armored knight dreaming of the two lovely ladies standing beside him. One lady, offering him a book and sword, symbolized the active life; the other, holding flowers, offered a life of pleasure.

THE KNIGHT'S DREAM, c. 1503-1504
National Gallery, London

The pupils in Viti's workshop talked about the pictures Perugino was painting on the walls of the stock exchange[1] in Perugia. Raphael remembered his father's genial friend, who used to visit Guidobaldo's court, and he longed to see the paintings. So Guidobaldo asked Perugino to hire Raphael as an assistant.

A few days later Raphael was riding up a winding road leading to the walled town of Perugia. It was exciting to think that he would soon be working with one of Italy's best-known artists. He found Perugino in the stock exchange. The master climbed down clumsily from the scaffolding to welcome Giovanni's son. He had grown fat, but Perugino's piercing black eyes were as bright as ever as he explained to his assistant what he was to paint. Then Raphael took his place on the scaffolding and started to work.

So absorbed was he in his painting that he scarcely listened to the other assistants, who talked about the fights between two families in Perugia. They told how Atalanta Baglioni cursed her son for murdering his brother, and how, two days later, she saw that son stabbed to death in the public square. How different this town was from peaceful Urbino.

Perugino, watching his new assistant at work, realized that soon the boy would be designing his own pictures.

Three years later seventeen-year-old Raphael set out for Città di Castello to fill his first commission. As he rode he planned the picture he would paint, an illustration of the coronation of Saint Nicholas. At the top of the big altarpiece would be God, between Saint Augustine and the Virgin Mary. Beneath would be Saint Nicholas trampling on the devil. First he would make careful drawings of each figure.

Raphael sketched models dressed in tights. He drew heads, hands, and drapery. He filled the empty pages in sketchbooks brought from Urbino. Using a page on which he had drawn some swans and a section of the duke's palace, he made a study of a man's head and noted a piece of drapery.

In the summer of 1501 the altarpiece was finished. Raphael put the money he had earned into his pocket and returned to Perugia.

1. Collegio del Campo

DRAWING FOR CORONATION OF SAINT NICHOLAS OF TOLENTINO, c. 1500
Musée des Beaux-Arts, Lille

Perugino's assistants were still talking about the rivalry between the Baglioni families. Atalanta was overwhelmed with grief for the loss of the son she had cursed, but the fighting between families continued. Almost every day there were clashes in the streets. During these violent days Raphael painted quietly in Perugino's studio. He loved to work on his master's paintings, which were restful pictures of saints and Madonnas placed far back in peaceful landscapes.

A church in Perugia commissioned Raphael to paint a *Coronation of the Virgin,* and from Città di Castello came another commission for an altarpiece. This was a picture of the crucifixion, which he painted in Perugino's studio. Raphael had often made copies of his master's crucifixion drawings and he used these drawings when he composed his altarpiece. He did not show the crucifixion as it really happened. The three Marys and Saint Jerome, who were grouped around the cross, did not grieve. Nor did Raphael show the agonies of Christ's death. This picture reflected the sweetness of Perugino's paintings and was filled with the fresh serenity of the younger painter.

THE CRUCIFIXION, c. 1502–1503
National Gallery, London

The name of Raphael of Urbino was now well known in Città di Castello. Many had seen the handsome young artist when he visited the city and more had admired his paintings, which hung in two of their churches. They were anxious to see the altarpiece commissioned for a third church, which Raphael was painting in Perugino's studio. The panel, nearly six feet high, showing *The Marriage of the Virgin,* would hang in Saint Joseph's chapel. Perugino had just finished a picture of the same subject for the cathedral in Perugia. Raphael knew the picture well, for he had helped his master paint some of the figures.

Following Perugino's plan, he grouped the figures in the foreground, placing the ring which Joseph offered to his bride in the center of the group. On the left stood Mary and her attendants. Joseph and his followers, carrying rods, stood on the right. One young man, a disappointed suitor, broke his rod because it had not blossomed. In the background a tiled pavement stretched to the horizon where a round temple reared majestically against a blue sky. Above the central arch Raphael signed his name, RAPHAEL VRBINAS, and below on either side he wrote the date in Roman numerals.

Raphael examined the finished painting. The figures were posed in the graceful but affected manner of his master. He had opened up the background, letting light and air into the picture, but it seemed to Raphael that the spacious landscape and domed temple, so like the one in Perugino's picture, looked more important than the figures in the foreground. He realized that he had much to learn.

Perugino's pictures for the stock exchange were finished. The master had returned to his home in Florence, where he was busy filling commissions. Raphael longed to join him in this city where Italy's best artists lived and worked. He had heard about the battle scenes which Leonardo da Vinci and the young sculptor Michelangelo were painting for the Town Hall[1]. He might even receive commissions in this prosperous city if the Duchess of Urbino would give him a letter to the governor of Florence.

---

1. Palazzo Vecchio

MARRIAGE OF THE VIRGIN, c. 1504
Brera Gallery, Milan

One fall day in 1504 Raphael rode into the Arno Valley. The river below wound like a shining ribbon between green banks. In the distance he could see the outline of Florence's cathedral dome and the graceful bell tower looming above a cluster of tiled roofs.

He put his hand in his pocket. The duchess' letter was still there. It was comforting to think that he had an introduction to the governor of this big city.

"The bearer of this note," it said, "will be Raphael, painter of Urbino, who, possessing great genius in his profession, has decided to live in Florence for a while. I am extremely attached to him and wish him to become a perfect painter." Would he find commissions, Raphael wondered as he rode through the city on his way to Perugino's studio.

Perugino welcomed his young friend enthusiastically. In his master's studio Raphael met many painters. It was exciting to hear them discuss the battle scenes which Florence's two great artists were designing. Perugino took him to Leonardo's studio. Raphael watched fascinated as the handsome artist, immaculately dressed, brought warriors and rearing horses to life. With quick strokes of his pen Raphael sketched one of these horsemen in his notebook.

Perugino took him to another studio where a young man with a crooked nose and dirty hands, dressed in a rumpled tunic, was painting another battle scene. The artist glared rudely when Raphael stepped up to admire the magnificently drawn nude figures. They looked as if they had been carved, Raphael thought, like the statue of David which he had admired in the city square. He marveled that Michelangelo could portray this rounded form on paper.

Raphael visited many studios in Florence. From each he learned something new. Older artists were impressed by Raphael's intelligence and charm, but the twenty-year-old artist from Urbino received no commissions. Too poor to hire models, he painted a portrait of himself. This frail youth with big brown eyes knew that he must learn more before he could succeed in Florence. A few months later Raphael set off for Perugia.

SELF-PORTRAIT, c. 1506
Uffizi Gallery, Florence

When Raphael returned to Perugia he studied the sketches he had made in Florence. How different these were from the ones he had made before. He had learned to show the rounded form of the human figure. The Madonnas looked more like real people than the affected Virgins he had drawn in Perugino's workshop. Backgrounds and buildings had disappeared. Mother and child were the only subjects of these pictures. He had imitated the soft shading of Leonardo's paintings and the sad, tender expression of his Madonnas.

It was this feeling that Raphael expressed in a Madonna he painted soon after he returned to Perugia. People were moved by its beauty. Some even believed it could work miracles. Three hundred years later a grand duke bought the painting and wherever he went he took the picture with him. Today *The Madonna of the Grand Duke* is one of the most loved of Raphael's pictures.

Commissions for Madonnas started to pour into Raphael's studio. Some came from Florence, and more from Perugia. Back and forth Raphael traveled, filling orders in the two cities. He completed one big altarpiece in Perugia and then, just as he was about to leave for Florence, Atalanta Baglioni commissioned him to paint an altarpiece for her family chapel.

MADONNA OF THE GRAND DUKE, c. 1505
Pitti Palace, Florence

Atalanta Baglioni could not forget the day she saw the son whom she had cursed murdered in the public square of Perugia. As atonement for her guilt she commissioned Raphael to paint an altarpiece in his memory. Raphael was honored to receive this important order and offered to make a drawing for the altarpiece while he was in Florence. During the eighty-mile trip from Perugia he thought about the subject for this picture, which would express a mother's grief for the loss of her son.

As soon as he arrived in Florence he made a drawing of the Virgin mourning over the dead Christ. Jesus' head rested on the lap of his grief-stricken mother; his knees were supported by Mary Magdalene. Mourners stood on either side. He made another sketch, arranging the figures in a different way. He copied other artists' pictures of this subject. He made sketches of corpses in the morgue. In the evenings when his studio was too dark to work on paintings of Madonnas, he drew by candlelight, trying to find new ways to express a mother's grief.

He was impressed by the vigor of Michelangelo's drawings, and after he had studied them he tried a new composition for his altarpiece, bringing more action into the picture.

He hired models and grouped them as if they were carrying the body of Christ to the tomb. He studied how they walked under the strain of the weight they bore. This group would be in the center of the picture. On the right he drew the Virgin fainting in the arms of her followers, just as Atalanta fainted when she saw her murdered son. Raphael divided the drawing into squares so that it could be transferred to a wooden panel, then rolled it up and set off for Perugia.

ENTOMBMENT DRAWING, c. 1506
British Museum, London

Raphael hired assistants to help him paint his picture of the entombment. Before the altarpiece was finished he was called back to Florence. The assistants continued with the work, and when Raphael returned to Perugia the finished painting was hanging in the Baglioni Chapel. The picture was disappointing. The violent pulling movement of the men was exaggerated, the fainting Virgin was too dramatic. Only the background seemed successful. In this peaceful landscape there was the note of harmony which pervaded Raphael's other pictures.

ENTOMBMENT, c. 1507
Borghese Gallery, Rome

Raphael sometimes stopped in Urbino when he traveled between Florence and Perugia. Duke Guidobaldo always welcomed him cordially and commissioned him to paint portraits of the members of his court. It was there he came to know the ambassador from Mantua, gracious, scholarly Baldassare Castiglione. The ambassador, five years older than Raphael, was impressed by the young talented artist who had the manner of a perfect courtier.

Castiglione was charmed by Raphael's little painting of Saint George, which Duke Guidobaldo was sending to the King of England. The duke, who had just received England's Order of the Garter, wished to repay King Henry for this honor.

The picture showed Saint George astride a rearing horse like the one Raphael had copied from Leonardo's battle scene. On the blue ribbon which circled the saint's left leg was lettered HONI, the first word of the motto for England's Order of the Garter.

When Baldassare Castiglione set off for the court of Henry VII in the spring of 1506, he took with him Raphael's little painting of the patron saint of England.

SAINT GEORGE, c. 1505
National Gallery of Art, Washington DC

When Raphael returned to Florence he visited the Town Hall where Leonardo, exquisitely groomed as ever, sat on a scaffolding transferring his battle scene to one of the walls. Raphael was dazzled by the glowing colors, more brilliant than the other frescoes he had seen. Leonardo, always interested in experiments, had decided to try a new paint mixed with oil. The young artist watched fascinated as the older artist painted the head of a screaming warrior.

Raphael found Michelangelo in his studio working furiously on his drawing of a battle scene. He growled when Raphael entered and went on with his work. His picture of powerful nude figures in action impressed the artist from Urbino. He took out his sketchbook and copied some of the figures. How much he could learn from these two great artists, he thought as he walked back to his studio and started to work on a Madonna he had been commissioned to paint for his friend Taddeo Taddei.

Taddeo Taddei, wealthy patron of the arts, was quick to recognize young talent. From thirty-year-old Michelangelo he ordered a Virgin carved in marble, and from Raphael, eight years younger, a painting of a Madonna. So attracted was he by Raphael's quiet charm that he asked the artist to visit him while he was in Florence.

Raphael made many sketches before he was ready to paint this picture for his friend. The Madonna would not be the sad distant mother he had painted before, but a real mother such as he had seen in Florence, sitting in a field watching her son at play. Raphael sketched the mother, her child, and the little Saint John many times. He arranged the three figures in different ways. He thought of Leonardo's painting of the Virgin and Saint Anne and how the artist had built the figures in the form of a pyramid. This was the composition he decided to use in his painting, and Taddei was delighted. The Madonna's beautiful head formed the peak of the triangle. In the background Taddei recognized the river, fields, and hills of the Arno Valley melting into the clear blue sky above.

MADONNA OF THE MEADOW, c. 1505-1506
Kunsthistorisches Museum, Vienna

The wealthy merchants who saw Raphael's Madonna hanging in Taddeo Taddei's house were eager to have one of the young artist's paintings. While other Florentine artists were covering whole walls with enormous pictures filled with many figures, Raphael painted small canvases for private houses. Some people commissioned Madonnas, others wished to have their portraits painted.

The prosperous wool merchant, Agnolo Doni, asked Raphael to paint a portrait of his wife. When the artist sat before his model he was reminded of a portrait he had seen in Leonardo's studio. The woman's tranquil pose and mysterious smile had haunted him. He had made sketches of the figure and the soft landscape background. Raphael showed Maddalena Doni, hands folded placidly in her lap, just as Leonardo had shown the Mona Lisa.

So delighted was Agnolo with the picture that he commissioned a portrait of himself. Raphael painted the thirty-year-old merchant exactly as he was with his thick black hair, big nose, and stern expression. Agnolo was so pleased with the perfect likeness that gave the portrait to his wife.

AGNOLO DONI, c. 1504-1507
Uffizi Gallery, Florence

MADDALENA DONI, c. 1504-1507
Uffizi Gallery, Florence

One of Raphael's many friends and patrons was Lorenzo Nasi, art lover and connoisseur. When Lorenzo was married in 1506, Raphael decided to paint a Madonna as a present for his friend.

First he sketched a mother who was trying to read as her child, standing between her knees, reached out to turn the pages of her book. Raphael was not satisfied with this arrangement. On the same sheet of paper he made a larger drawing, placing the baby on the mother's lap. Her book had disappeared. The baby reached for a bird which little Saint John had brought him. The figure of the mother was unclothed, showing the position of the model's legs as she sat with the baby in her lap. Raphael took another sheet of paper. Again he drew the child standing between his mother's knees, his foot resting on hers. Once more the baby reached for his mother's book, but he was more interested in the bird Saint John was holding. This arrangement seemed more pleasing, the pyramid more compact. But as soon as Raphael started to enlarge the drawing on canvas he made changes in the composition.

DRAWINGS FOR MADONNA OF THE GOLDFINCH, c. 1505
Ashmolean Museum, Oxford

Publisher's Note: R.V. was Raphael's signature, short for Raphael Vrbinas.

The picture which Raphael gave to his friend Lorenzo Nasi showed the Madonna with a book in her left had. Saint John, holding the goldfinch he had caught, rested his hands on the Virgin's knee, and the Christ Child, no longer interested in his mother's book, reached out to smooth the bird's head.

This Madonna, like the one Raphael had painted for Taddeo Taddei, had brought her child out into the country to play. The fields and streams of the Arno Valley stretched behind her. The cathedral dome and bell tower rising above the walls of Florence were silhouetted against distant mountains.

Many years later, Nasi's painting was badly damaged when the house where it hung collapsed. Other artists restored it. Although much of Raphael's careful work has disappeared, the serene harmony of this *Madonna of the Goldfinch* still remains.

MADONNA OF THE GOLDFINCH, c. 1505-1506
Uffizi Gallery, Florence

The people of Florence never saw the battle scenes which their two great artists had planned for the Town Hall. Leonardo, impatient because his oil colors did not dry, lighted a stove under his painting. His assistants watched horrified as the colors started to melt, and soon Leonardo's picture was a mass of brilliant streaks running down the wall. The doors of the Town Hall were closed, and Leonardo set off for Milan. The year before, Michelangelo had put aside his drawing of a battle scene in order to fill a commission for Pope Julius. He was now in Rome designing a monumental tomb for this mighty Pope.

Raphael remained in Florence painting Madonnas for merchants' houses. Once again he painted a Virgin with Jesus and Saint John. The Christ Child nestling against his mother's knee looked up affectionately as he reached for her book. Saint John, kneeling on the Virgin's left, gazed adoringly at the Christ Child. Once again Raphael showed a background of fields, river, and hills melting into a blue sky, but the distant town did not look like Florence. Its peaked roofs and pointed spires belonged to some northern city which Raphael had seen in another artist's picture.

From Rome came news that Michelangelo had been ordered to stop his work on Julius' tomb so that he could decorate the ceiling of the Pope's chapel. Raphael wished that he had such big surfaces to cover. He wrote to his uncle in Urbino, telling of his plan to go to Rome and asking for a letter of recommendation from the duke. The uncle's answer brought bad news. Duke Guidobaldo was dead.

"I could not really read your letter without tears," Raphael replied.

But the duchess did not forget Giovanni Santi's son. She wrote to her relative, Pope Julius, to remind him of the young artist's talent. Julius heard Raphael's name again from Bramante of Urbino, architect of the Pope's church in Rome. Michelangelo spoke of the young artist too. So angry was he that he had been forced to give up his sculpture in order to decorate the chapel ceiling that he recommended Raphael for the job. But Julius had other plans for the young artist from Urbino.

In the summer of 1508 the Pope summoned Raphael to Rome to decorate the apartments in his palace.

LA BELLE JARDINIÈRE, c. 1507
Louvre, Paris

Julius strode through the small high-ceilinged rooms of his apartment, pointing with his cane to the spaces he wanted Raphael to decorate. The paintings that were there must go, he ordered. The artists had been dismissed. Raphael of Urbino was now in charge of decorating the Pope's *stanze,* or apartments.

Raphael looked at the walls pierced with doors and windows and the vaulted ceilings stretching down to the corners. Never had he hoped to have such big surfaces to cover. He stood for some time in the library. The pictures in this room, where papal documents were signed, should be dedicated to literature, law, philosophy, and religion, Raphael decided.

He talked of his plans to Bramante and asked the advice of scholars, architects, and philosophers he met at his friend's home. To help him plan the work, he hired some of the artists Julius had dismissed. While Michelangelo, unable to bear the company of assistants, painted alone in the Sistine Chapel, Raphael started to work with a host of admiring helpers. Not wishing to destroy the pictures Julius had condemned, he asked assistants to make copies before they were erased.

Julius was delighted with the plans Raphael showed him. In each pointed corner joining walls and ceiling was a figure framed in a round medallion. These figures, representing poetry, law, philosophy, and religion, were keys to the pictures in the vaulting above and the walls below. Underneath theology was a picture glorifying the Church. In the lower section a row of Christian fathers discussed the Holy Trinity and, above, the Trinity and saints were seated on a bank of clouds. Julius was impressed by the carefully worked out composition and ordered Raphael to start work immediately.

While assistants enlarged the drawing, Raphael made careful studies of each section of his picture. He always carried a notebook, jotting down things he wanted to remember. He sketched front and back views of a figure leaning on a railing and made a study of a foreshortened foot. On the same page he wrote a love sonnet to a beautiful girl he had met in Rome. Soon assistants began transferring Raphael's drawing to the library wall, while Julius waited impatiently to see the finished painting.

SKETCHES FOR DISPUTA, c. 1508-1509
British Museum, London

As Raphael's painting came to life Julius marveled that the walls of his library seemed to open out. How skillfully the young artist had divided up the space! How beautifully he had brought heaven and earth together by placing the altar which held the Holy Sacrament in the center of the picture. Poets, scholars, philosophers, and popes were gathered around the altar to worship this symbol of the Christian Church. Julius recognized the courtyard of Saint Peter's Church, which Bramante was designing. He recognized Bramante too, leaning on a railing at the left, as he explained what he was reading to his pupils. Some of his pupils pointed toward the altar, to show that the Christian faith transcended man's learning.

On the step above, another scientist had flung aside his book, while his pupils fell on their knees to worship the Trinity. On the right stood Julius' uncle, Pope Sixtus IV, who had built the chapel Michelangelo was decorating. Behind him was Italy's great poet, Dante, wearing a wreath of laurel. Saint Thomas Aquinas stood next to the altar pointing to the Trinity in heaven, where Christ sat enthroned between God and the Holy Ghost. On His right was the Virgin Mary and on the left Saint John the Baptist.

A bank of clouds swelled out to the edges of the domed heaven, and on these clouds sat the fathers of the church. On the far left sat Saint Peter next to Adam, then Saint John the Evangelist writing busily. Next came King David, Saint Lawrence, and, half hidden by a cloud, the prophet Jeremiah. Saint Paul sat on the far right next to Abraham, then Saint James, and Moses holding the tablets of the Ten Commandments. Next came Saint Stephen, and last Judah Maccabee in shining armor.

Julius followed the progress of the picture enthusiastically. Raphael was never too busy to discuss his plans. Long before the painting glorifying the church was finished, Raphael showed Julius the drawings he was making for the opposite wall.

DISPUTE OF THE HOLY SACRAMENT (DISPUTA), c. 1509-1510
Vatican, Rome

Julius examined the drawing Raphael unrolled in front of him. Here was the subject the Pope had chosen to face the picture glorifying religion. Beneath the figure of philosophy, Raphael had glorified science and learning. Julius studied every detail excitedly. Scholars and scientists of ancient Greece were gathered in a majestic building. Under the central arch two philosophers stepped forward, talking as they walked. Aristotle, hand extended, showed that man's wisdom came from the world about him. Plato pointed upward to show that man's inspiration came from heaven. One either side scholars listened thoughtfully or argued heatedly. In the courtyard in the foreground, scientists worked busily. On the left Pythagoras solved a mathematical problem in his book. On the right Euclid, compass in hand, illustrated a problem in geometry. Ptolemy, holding a globe, lectured on astronomy. The plan was impressive and Julius ordered Raphael to start work at once.

Almost every day Julius visited the library and his private chapel to check on the progress of the decorations. Michelangelo, lying on the scaffolding under the chapel ceiling, refused to let Julius see his paintings. Julius, enraged, ordered the scaffolding removed. He was overwhelmed by the grandeur of the paintings high above him. Raphael came to look and marveled at the vigor of Michelangelo's heroic figures painted in sweeping brush strokes. When he returned to the *stanza* and started to paint, his own brush strokes became freer and his figures took on a new vitality.

He painted rapidly, completing a figure in a day. Julius was excited to see each come to life, for many were portraits of people of his day. Plato with long flowing beard and hair had the noble features of Leonardo da Vinci. Julius recognized Bramante's bald head bent over his compass and young Raphael himself was standing on the extreme right of the picture. A youth in white, standing behind Pythagoras, was Julius' nephew, the young Duke of Urbino. In the center a stocky man rested his elbow on a block of marble. This figure, which had not appeared in Raphael's drawing, was the artist's tribute to Michelangelo's glorious paintings.

SCHOOL OF ATHENS, c. 1509-1511
Vatican, Rome

Julius shielded his eyes from the light streaming through the library window. As he grew accustomed to the darkness he could see the picture above him. Framed in a round medallion was a winged woman's figure representing poetry. Her lovely head, crowned with laurel, was slightly turned. In one hand she held a lyre, in the other a book. On either side was a cupid holding a plaque inscribed with the Latin words *Numine afflatur,* meaning "Inspiration from above."

Still shielding his eyes, Julius examined the painting underneath this figure, a beautiful picture glorifying poetry.

Publisher's Note: This photograph of the ceiling of the Vatican's *Stanza della Segnatura,* Room of the Signatura, contains four medallions, clockwise from the top, representing Justice, Philosophy, Poetry, and Theology.

POETRY, c. 1509
Vatican, Rome

Apollo, surrounded by Muses, sat on Mount Parnassus playing an instrument similar to a violin. Raphael had arranged the picture around a window so that the opening seemed to give height to the hill above it. Blind Homer dictated verses to a youth beside him. Behind was Virgil, who was showing Dante the mountain of the gods. Below sat Sappho, resting her elbow on the window frame, while on the other side the Greek poet Pindar talked with Horace and another poet. Above stood a bearded man looking over his shoulder. His sad eyes were those of Michelangelo, sculptor, painter, and also poet. The pale blue sky, green trees and grass, and the soft lilac robes blended harmoniously, making a restful pattern on the wall.

Julius turned to the opposite wall to examine Raphael's picture glorifying justice. Pope Gregory IX sat on his throne issuing decrees to his cardinals. Assistants were still working on the picture, but Julius was able to recognize the people in the painting. The stern-looking Pope with white hair and beard was not Gregory, who had lived two hundred years before. The Pope sitting on his throne was an excellent likeness of Julius II, and standing beside him were cardinals of Julius' day.

Julius was delighted. How wise he had been to choose young Raphael to decorate his apartment, he thought as he strode into the next room where the artist was working.

PARNASSUS, c. 1509-1511
Vatican, Rome

Raphael climbed down from the scaffolding to greet the Pope. Julius looked old and tired. He asked impatiently when he could see the picture. Raphael assured him that the painting was almost finished. Julius shaded his eyes again and looked at the space above the window. Between the platforms of the scaffolding he could see a picture of himself kneeling before an altar. His strong sharp profile looked heavy but still vigorous. At the other side of the altar a priest in a blue and gold robe celebrated mass. Cardinals and priests stood on the steps behind the Pope, and kneeling below were five of the Swiss Guards in brightly colored uniforms, one of which was Raphael. Opposite was a group of women who had come to hear the mass.

Raphael showed Julius his plans for the other walls. In each drawing Julius recognized himself, shown as he wished to be, a forceful Pope, defender of the Faith and leader of the Church Triumphant. He urged Raphael to hire more assistants so that the work could progress quickly. Then as Raphael climbed back on the scaffolding, Julius, leaning heavily of his cane, set off for the Sistine Chapel.

THE MASS AT BOLSENA, c. 1512–1514
Vatican, Rome

The tortured Michelangelo had lain on the scaffolding under the chapel ceiling for four years painting monumental figures which told the story of the creation. Then in the fall of 1512 he wrote his father in Florence:

"I have finished the chapel which I have been painting. The Pope is very satisfied."

Raphael was moved by the vigor and action in Michelangelo's picture. He began to work with renewed energy. He pictured an exciting story from the Bible—Heliodorus had been sent to rob a church when a knight on horseback appeared in the sky, followed by two youths with switches. Just as the angels of vengeance drove the robber from the temple, the Pope, carried on a chair, entered the place of worship. This Pope, representing the Church Triumphant, was Julius II, who had just driven the French from Italy. Raphael's portrait was a perfect likeness—a strong profile with beetling brows over deep-set eyes and a white beard which he had vowed not to shave until the French had been driven from Italian soil.

While Raphael hurried to finish the other figures, Julius lay ill in the next room. He called Raphael to his bedside. He wanted to see the *stanze* finished before he died, and he asked Raphael to start decorating the corridor leading to his private rooms. Raphael wondered how he could find time to take on another commission, but he graciously agreed to do as the Pope ordered. Returning to the picture of Heliodorus, he quickly painted the figures of the people carrying the Pope's chair. In front was a bearded man, an artist friend who had made many engravings of Raphael's paintings. On the other side was a portrait of one of his assistants, and in the foreground he painted a likeness of himself. Then while his assistants were working on the figures of Heliodorus and the avenging angels, Raphael began designing decorations for the Pope's loggia.

HELIODORUS CHASED FROM THE TEMPLE, c. 1511-1512
Vatican, Rome

Work in the *stanze* progressed slowly, for the slightest noise disturbed the Pope, who lay desperately ill in the next room. From time to time Raphael and his assistants had to stop painting. Payments for the work came less and less often, but Raphael continued to plan decorations for the Pope's loggia. He accepted commissions from bankers and merchants so that he could pay his assistants.

A scaffolding had been built opposite the picture of *Heliodorus Chased from the Temple*. On this wall Raphael was painting another picture which glorified the Pope. He had chosen an event in Roman history. One thousand years before, Attila, King of the Huns, had conquered most of Italy. As his army marched toward Rome, Pope Leo rode out to meet the invaders and persuaded the barbarian to turn back. Once again Raphael pictured the Pope as symbol of the Church Triumphant.

Raphael must have thought of Leonardo's battle scene when he painted the rearing horses and screaming warriors of Attila's army. The right half of the painting showed tumult and confusion, while on the left the Pope, mounted on a white horse, rode majestically into the picture.

Only a few of the charging horsemen had been finished when Julius II died. A new Pope sat on the throne in Rome. Fat jovial Leo X knew Raphael well. He had admired Raphael's paintings of Madonnas in Florence, for Leo was a member of that city's ruling family and, like the other Medici, was a lover of the arts. He urged Raphael to finish the *stanze* as soon as possible, for he had many commissions for the young artist from Urbino.

Raphael painted the figure of the Pope turning away Attila's army, but it was not a portrait of Julius II or of the Leo who had stopped the Hun's invasion. This Pope riding on a white horse had the pudgy face and well-groomed hands of Raphael's new patron, Leo X.

While assistants completed the figures of the Pope's escorts and Saint Peter and Saint Paul appearing in the sky, Raphael, seated on a scaffolding in the same room, was painting a glowing scene around the window of another wall.

MEETING OF SAINT LEO AND ATTILA, c. 1513-1514
Vatican, Rome

Raphael could not forget the luminous picture by Piero della Francesca which had once decorated the wall where he was painting. Regretfully he had followed Julius' orders to destroy it. This glowing painting outshone the daylight from the window it surrounded. It was this brilliance that Raphael tried to equal in his painting, *The Deliverance of Saint Peter.* Here was a new problem which Raphael solved alone. Sometimes his pupils stopped work in order to marvel at their master's brush strokes, which seemed to illuminate the dark space around the window.

Above he showed Saint Peter's cell flooded with a blinding light which came from the angel who had just alighted. The rays were reflected in the armor of the soldiers standing on either side and played on the sleeping figure of Saint Peter. On the steps outside the cell soldiers recoiled in terror, while on the opposite side the luminous angel guided Saint Peter past the sleeping guards

Raphael painted rapidly but he was frequently interrupted. He often had to put aside his brushes in order to check on the progress of the Pope's loggia, or fill an order for a Madonna. The prosperous banker Chigi commissioned him to paint figures on the ceiling of his family chapel. They were monumental figures like those Michelangelo had painted in the Pope's chapel.

"All that Raphael learned about art he learned from me," Michelangelo growled when he saw the pictures.

But the people of Rome were impressed by this handsome, talented artist whom they used to see on his way to work, followed by admiring friends and pupils. One day as Raphael and his friends crossed the cathedral square, Michelangelo, crooked, disheveled, and alone, was walking down the steps of Saint Peter's. He stared at Raphael and his followers. "You look like a prince instead of a painter," he said fiercely.

"And *you* look like an executioner," Raphael replied calmly as he and his admirers passed by.

DELIVERANCE OF SAINT PETER, c. 1514
Vatican, Rome

On the bank of the river Tiber, not far from the Pope's palace, stood Agostino Chigi's summer home, Villa Farnesina. In the beautiful dining room, which had once been stables, he gave elaborate banquets. People told of how, when Pope Leo was a guest, the gold and silver plates were tossed into the Tiber after the Pope had eaten.

Raphael visited Chigi's villa often, for Chigi had commissioned him to decorate a gallery on the lower floor. On warm days he walked along the riverbank on his way to Chigi's house. He loved to see children playing outside the peasant cottages and mothers sunning in the doorways, holding their babies in their laps. One pretty mother, wearing the brightly colored shawl and headdress of a Roman peasant, caught his eye. He sketched her in his notebook. The pose of the child's body pressed against his mother's breast, the tilt of the mother's head and the curve of her embracing arms, made one continuous circle. How beautifully this picture would fit the round frame so popular in Italy at that time, Raphael thought. He noted the bright colors of the mother's peasant costume, the blue dress with bright red sleeves, and her green and red striped shawl.

A few days later Raphael found time to make a painting from his sketch. The dark-haired mother sat in a chair holding her child, whose head was the center of the circle. Standing at the mother's knee was young Saint John, with his face and hands directed toward the Christ Child.

This Roman mother, who was called the *Madonna of the Chair,* is one of the most loved of all of Raphael's Madonna paintings.

MADONNA OF THE CHAIR, c. 1513–1514
Pitti Palace, Florence

Raphael often dined with his old friend Castiglione, who had moved to Rome. At Castiglione's house he came to know Cardinal Bibbiena of Urbino—poet, writer, and secretary to Pope Leo. He made friends with the classical scholar Cardinal Bembo, who loved to suggest subjects for Raphael's pictures. Bembo often quoted from the Florentine poet Politian, who had once been Castiglione's teacher. He recited Politian's poem about the nymph Galatea sailing across the sea on a shell drawn by dolphins. He imagined how Raphael could picture this scene on a long wall of Chigi's gallery. Raphael had seen the subject carved in stone on the wall of another palace. How beautiful this would be in color! He pictured in his mind nymphs, tritons, and cupids against clear blue sea and sky.

Raphael's painting showed Galatea, having escaped the Cyclops, riding triumphantly in her seashell chariot. She looked backward as she rode, her rose robe floating behind her. All about her centaurs and tritons plunged through the water, embracing the nymphs they had captured. Three cupids floated in the azure sky, aiming their arrows at the beautiful Galatea.

Bembo was charmed by Raphael's picture. Castiglione's enthusiasm was even greater. Raphael could not accept their praise.

"As for Galatea," he wrote to Castiglione, "I would consider myself a great master if she has even one half the qualities your lordship finds in it."

Raphael never finished the decorations for Chigi's palace, for he was constantly called away to fill commissions for the Pope.

GALATEA, c. 1512
Villa Farnesina, Rome

"His Holiness has given me three hundred gold ducats in advance," Raphael wrote to his uncle in 1514, "because I am to be attached to the fabric of Saint Peter's."

Raphael's old friend Bramante had died, and Leo had appointed the painter to design the most important church in Christendom.

"You were considered by Bramante to be so skilled in architecture," Leo wrote, "that he, when dying, spoke of you as worthy to succeed him."

Raphael could not refuse so great an honor, although he was already overwhelmed with work. "I hope I shall not sink under it," he wrote to Castiglione. Other artists complained that a painter could not be an architect. "But," wrote Raphael, "the model which I have made pleases His Holiness."

While workmen tore down the old Saint Peter's, Raphael continued to decorate the Pope's apartments.

"I have already begun to paint a new room for His Holiness," Raphael wrote to his uncle. The pictures illustrated stories from the lives of Popes named Leo. The first showed how one Pope stopped a fire in Rome which threatened to destroy Saint Peter's. In the foreground women knelt in prayer or clung to their children. Some carried jugs of water, one man tried to scale a wall, and another carried an old man on his back. Pope Leo, standing on a balcony of Saint Peter's, raised his hand in blessing. Below, people marveled at the miracle. Raphael worked on many of the nude figures in this painting, while his pupils completed the other pictures.

Raphael often discussed his work with Cardinal Bibbiena. So attached was the cardinal to the young artist that he decided Raphael would make a fine husband for his niece.

"She is a beautiful young girl of the best reputation," Raphael wrote, but he was too busy to plan an early wedding with Maria Bibbiena. He was painting an altarpiece for a church in Bologna, checking on the decorations for the loggia, and even found time to decorate the cardinal's bathroom. Almost every day he consulted with architects and builders about the construction of Saint Peter's. Then one day Leo asked Raphael to come to the Sistine Chapel to discuss another commission he wanted the artist to undertake.

FIRE IN BORGO, c. 1514-1517
Vatican, Rome

Leo and Raphael, standing in the Sistine Chapel, looked up at the ceiling Michelangelo had decorated. Here was the story of mankind from the creation of the universe to the birth of Christ. On the walls were pictures by other artists illustrating scenes from the life of Moses and of Christ. Only the lives of Christ's apostles were missing from this history of the Christian world. Leo pointed to the spaces under the wall paintings. Here he wanted tapestries which would picture scenes from the lives of the apostles. Raphael must find time to design these tapestries, which would be woven by skilled workmen in Flanders.

A few days later Raphael was hard at work making sketches to illustrate the acts of the apostles, while his pupils prepared enormous sheets of paper, ten feet high, which were overlapped and pasted together. Then Raphael and his pupils, using thick gouache, started to create paintings for the tapestries. He pictured the stories exactly as the Bible told them. One showed how Christ sat in Simon Peter's boat and told the fishermen to let down their nets:

"And when they had done this, they enclosed a great multitude of fishes.... But when Simon Peter saw it, he fell down at Jesus' knees, saying, 'Depart from me; for I am a sinful man, O Lord.'"

Leo was impressed by the grandeur and action of the figures, so like those of Michelangelo. He admired the rich colors: the gray birds in the foreground and the shimmering blue sea in the background. What a brilliant spot this tapestry would make on the chapel wall.

Much care was devoted to these paintings, an unusually large portion of the work appears to be in Raphael's own hand. He also designed borders for the tapestries, showing scenes from the life of Leo X. Soon the paintings were on their way to Flanders. Three years later the tapestries were hung in the Sistine Chapel. People marveled at these pictures woven in threads of bright reds, blues, and glittering gold. They were impressed by their enormous cost. But they did not know that Raphael's paintings, which remained in Flanders, were far more beautiful than the tapestries.

MIRACULOUS DRAUGHT OF FISHES
Tapestry Cartoon, c. 1515-1516
Victoria and Albert Museum, London

As Raphael rode about Rome attending to his many duties he noticed that the stones of the ancient city were being used to make new buildings. He was troubled to see that the antique monuments were disappearing and he spoke of his concern to Leo. Soon Raphael was appointed by the Pope to supervise the preservation of ancient Rome.

Raphael spent many hours examining excavations. He made drawings of old buildings and measurements of Roman ruins. Scholarly Cardinal Bembo loved to accompany the young artist on his trips about the city, and Castiglione, steeped in the culture of ancient Rome, often joined his friend.

Castiglione's admiration for the young artist grew each day. Raphael's good looks and gentle manners, his intelligence and talent, and his modesty and thoughtfulness of others made him the ideal gentleman whom Castiglione described later in his book, *The Courtier*. He was delighted when Raphael found time to paint his portrait.

Castiglione sat dressed in a handsomely tailored black velvet tunic with gray sleeves. A big black hat framed his bearded face. The perfect gentleman never wore bright colors, Castiglione believed, because they would hide the true color of his inner self. The portrait, a beautiful harmony of silver tones, was a perfect likeness. Castiglione described it in a sonnet. As if his wife were writing him from Mantua, he told of her feeling for the painting:

"Your portrait painted by Raphael lightens my anxiety…your child recognizes it and greets it with stammers. By it, I console myself and charm the long days."

Raphael's many friends clamored to have their portraits painted.

"I have such a love of perfection," Cardinal Bembo wrote, "that I too have decided to have my portrait painted by Raphael." He spoke of Raphael's portrait of a mutual friend. "Raphael has painted our Tebaldeo so realistically," wrote the cardinal, "that the picture resembles him more than he himself."

BALDASSARE CASTIGLIONE, c. 1514-1515
Louvre, Paris

In the fall of 1517 Raphael moved into his new house not far from Saint Peter's Square. This handsome brick and cement palace had been designed by his friend Bramante. On the lower floor was a row of arches and on the floor above tall narrow windows divided by pairs of columns. Whenever he could, Raphael retired to his spacious house and, shut in his studio with its carved wooden ceiling, worked alone.

He soon forgot the many duties that burdened him as he painted a large altarpiece commissioned for Saint Sixtus' Chapel in the town of Piacenza. The picture showed a beautiful Madonna standing on a bank of clouds between Saint Sixtus and Saint Barbara. Two green curtains had just been pulled aside to reveal the holy vision to the saints. Saint Sixtus, in papal robes, gazed adoringly at the Virgin and her son, while Saint Barbara turned away, overwhelmed by the revelation. Two cherubs in the foreground seemed to be lost in contemplation.

The Madonna was dressed in simple robes. Her feet were bare; but, unlike the mothers Raphael had painted before, this Virgin seemed to have floated down from heaven. She was not burdened by the weight of the child she held. Her son was not a chubby baby clinging to his mother, but a serious child whose deep-set eyes were filled with sadness as if he foresaw his tragic fate. This was one of the last Madonnas Raphael ever painted.

Publisher's Note: *Sistine Madonna* was completed in 1514, making it improbable that Raphael worked on this piece while living in the house designed by Bramante.

SISTINE MADONNA, c. 1513-1514
Dresden Museum

Dressed in a red velvet cape lined with ermine and an ermine-lined cap on his head, Leo X sat for his portrait. Raphael knew his sitter well. This thickset man with full lips loved luxury. His flabby cheeks and sallow skin showed signs of overeating. His well-groomed hands held a magnifying glass, for Leo, like other members of the Medici family, was nearsighted. On the red tablecloth in front of him was a beautifully illuminated book, for Leo was a scholar and a passionate lover of the arts. He spent his money recklessly. His appetite for works of art could not be satisfied. Long before Raphael had completed one commission, Leo thought of another for his favorite artist.

Leo ordered decorations for his banquet room which would picture the life of the Emperor Constantine. He was delighted with Raphael's drawings for these decorations. They looked like tapestries hung between sets of columns. Always eager to try new methods, Raphael decided to use oil paints. The finished pictures, painted by assistants, were hard and shiny. They did not do justice to Raphael's magnificent compositions, for he had little time to supervise the work. He was asked to design stage sets for Leo's elaborate pageants and even had to paint a picture of the Pope's pet elephant, which was placed above a doorway of his palace. He was showered with commissions from Leo's relatives.

One Medici, a cardinal, asked him to design his villa, and Cardinal Giuliano de' Medici, whom Raphael painted standing behind Leo's chair, commissioned an altarpiece for a church in France. His friend Sebastiano del Piombo had been commissioned to paint a picture for the same church. Michelangelo, hoping to make Raphael's picture look inferior, offered to help Piombo paint his altarpiece.

"If Piombo allows himself to be helped by Michelangelo," Raphael said when he heard the news, "my victory will be all the greater." Then he shut himself in his studio and started to make drawings for his altarpiece.

LEO X WITH CARDINALS MEDICI AND ROSSI, c. 1518-20
Uffizi Gallery, Florence

Raphael's drawings illustrated two events in the life of Christ. He had often read the Bible story of Christ's transfiguration. It told how Christ took three of his apostles to a high mountaintop where he was transfigured before them, "so that his face did shine as the sun and his garments became white as light." As this miracle was taking place the other apostles were gathered at the foot of the mountain, where a man had brought his epileptic son to be cured.

Raphael made many sketches, working out a composition which would combine these two scenes. He made careful studies of each figure and beautiful drawings of apostles' heads and hands. He would paint this picture himself, for he must show Michelangelo that he could still create a work of art without the help of his assistants.

The quiet hours in his studio were happy ones for Raphael, but he was often interrupted. He spent days working on the restoration of Roman ruins. He planned a book with pictures of all the classical monuments. He invented an instrument to measure ruins, and drawings to show how ancient buildings should be restored.

"He is producing an admirable work," a friend wrote. "I refer to the town of Rome...which he almost reconstructed in its ancient grandeur. Nearly all people regard him as a god...but he is withal free from vanity, he is friendly toward everyone." He spoke of Raphael's kindness to a sick friend: "This old man is being nursed as a child by the very rich Raphael of Urbino." He gave board and lodging to many of his assistants. Soon his house was too small to hold his pupils and his work.

In the spring of 1520, Raphael bought a piece of land and started to design a bigger house, for in the summer he planned to marry Maria Bibbiena.

HEADS AND HANDS OF APOSTLES, Drawings for the Transfiguration, c. 1519-1520
Ashmolean Museum, Oxford

Cardinal Bibbiena was delighted when the date for Raphael's wedding was announced, but before the wedding plans were made Maria Bibbiena fell seriously ill. A few weeks later she died. The grief-stricken cardinal arranged a funeral for his niece, and a saddened Raphael gave directions for the building of Maria's tomb.

Raphael took many trips into the country that spring of 1520 to study the ruins outside Rome. The trips were tiring. One day he returned to his house and started to work on his painting of the transfiguration. The top part of the picture showed Christ floating in clouds between two prophets. Beneath were the three apostles who had fallen to the ground in amazement. At the foot of the mountain excited people begged the apostles who had stayed below to cure the epileptic child. Some apostles leaned forward, anxious to help, others pointed to the Christ transfigured, showing that help must come from heaven.

Raphael picked up a brush and painted the figure of Saint Andrew sitting in the foreground. When his studio grew too dark to paint he put aside his brushes and wrapped himself in his cloak. Suddenly he felt very cold.

The next day Raphael lay ill with a raging fever. His friends watched over him anxiously. Castiglione and Bembo sat by his bedside and Leo called often to bring his papal blessing. On the sixth of April, Raphael called a lawyer and made a will. He asked to be buried near Maria Bibbiena in the Pantheon, the only antique building not in ruins. A few hours later Raphael of Urbino died.

"Nothing is talked of here but the death of this excellent man who closed his first life at the age of thirty-seven," wrote the Mantuan ambassador. Mourning Romans filed into Raphael's house and gazed reverently at the unfinished picture of the transfiguration which hung above the artist's deathbed. Two pupils were commissioned to complete the altarpiece, and other assistants continued with the many unfinished works which Raphael left behind him.

"He gave promise of many great things," the Mantuan ambassador wrote, "but his renown, which is subject to neither time nor death, will be perpetual."

TRANSFIGURATION, c. 1516-1520
Vatican, Rome

www.ingramcontent.com/pod-product-compliance
Lightning Source LLC
Chambersburg PA
CBHW050754110526
44592CB00003B/58